MAY A CHRISTIAN BELIEVE IN REINCARNATION?

May a Christian Believe in Reincarnation?

BY ABBOT GEORGE BURKE
(SWAMI NIRMALANANDA GIRI)

&

The Necessity for Reincarnation

BY ANNIE BESANT

LIGHT OF THE SPIRIT
PRESS
CEDAR CREST, NEW MEXICO

Second Edition

Published by
Light of the Spirit Press

Light of the Spirit Monastery
P. O. Box 1370
Cedar Crest, New Mexico 87008

www.OCOY.org

ISBN-13: 978-1523376292
ISBN-10: 1523376295

Library of Congress Control Number: 2016900944
CreateSpace Independent Publishing Platform, North Charleston, SC

Because of the dynamic nature of the Internet, any web addresses or links contained in this book may have changed since publication and may no longer be valid.

Cover art: A colorized version of a painting of Christ by the German painter Heinrich Hofmann (1824–1911)

The Necessity for Reincarnation by Annie Besant is in the public domain.

PREFACE

How this study came about

You might find the history of this study interesting and amusing.

Quite some time ago we became very good friends with an Eastern Orthodox archpriest who not only believed in reincarnation, but had engaged for years in research into methods of past-life recall. One afternoon he phoned and told me that several guests were coming from an Orthodox seminary to visit him and he planned to bring up the compatibility of reincarnation with Christianity. The reason for his call was to ask if the monks and I could research the subject of reincarnation in early Christianity to give him material to prove that Christians could believe in reincarnation. Certainly we would! For the next few days several of us went through our library and finally reported back to our friend that we had a lot of material for him to use.

Then he revealed to us that what brought this on was the discovery of a small boy in our state that remembered being his own uncle! And the priest had been asked by the local television station to comment on this at the end of their broadcast of the story. Were we ever excited. An Eastern Orthodox priest advocating reincarnation on television! So we delivered the material and awaited the broadcast.

The segment on the boy was very well done and very believable. Then suddenly there on the screen we saw our priest friend in full vestments standing at the front of his church. This was it!

No, it wasn't.

He began a tirade (no other word for it) about how Christians cannot believe in reincarnation and how incompatible the belief is with Christianity.

For us, the bottom dropped out. But when life hands you lemons, make lemonade, so I just worked all that researched material into a small book I named *May a Christian Believe in Reincarnation?* But the story was not finished.

I was working on one of the first PCs, a Franklin Ace with a floppy disk and a primitive dot matrix printer. Nobody had told me to save my work every day, so I did not. Nor had anyone told me to make a hard copy on the printer each day. So no hard copy.

Finally I felt I was done, so I did a save. The computer spewed everything over the disk and I had gibberish.

More lemons called for more lemonade, so I wrote the whole thing again, and it turned out better. But I still did not save or make a hard copy, and when I saved at the end.... It was the end. The same disaster happened.

It took a while to take it in, but–well, you know: lemons. So I wrote it a third time, and yes it was actually better. But the third time was not a charm: it was the same destruction. I did not make lemonade, I cried. Really. And then consoling myself with the idea (but no proof) that the third version had also been an improvement, I wrote it for a fourth time. No, I did not save. No, I did not make a printout.

I saved. The computer made the usual hash. Then a cynical thought came to me: What if this computer was lying to me? What if the text was not scattered all over the disk like the directory showed? What if it would print out?

It did. So now you have the book. The lemonade come from some very sour lemons, but I hope you will find it sweet.

MAY A CHRISTIAN BELIEVE IN REINCARNATION?

O ur purpose in this brief study is to determine if, in good conscience, a Christian may believe in reincarnation. In ancient orthodox Jewish and Christian writings, as well as the Holy Scriptures, we can find reincarnation–also known as the transmigration of souls–as a fully developed belief. Consequently as Orthodox Jews Jesus and the Apostles would have been familiar with the belief in rebirth.

My favorite comment on the subject of reincarnation is that given by the Roman Catholic Capuchin stigmatist Saint Padre Pio. When one of his spiritual daughters was "told on" for believing in reincarnation, he told her accusers very firmly: "It does not matter what you believe about reincarnation. The only thing that matters is this: Are you seeking for God now?"

A Catholic cardinal speaks

Just what do we mean by reincarnation? Cardinal Mercier (1851-1926) of the Roman Catholic Church, an eminent scholar and theologian of the conservative Christian Tradition, in his book *Psychologie* gives this definition of three views of reincarnation:

> "Under the term *Wiedermenschwerdung*, metempsychosis, or the transmigration of souls, a great variety of ideas may be understood: either a series of repetitions of existence under the twofold condition that the soul maintains consciousness of its personality and that there is a final unit in the series of transmigrations; or a series of repetitions of existence without any final unit, and yet with the presupposition that the soul maintains consciousness of its personality; or, finally, an endless series of repetitions of existence with the loss of consciousness of personal identity....*So far as concerns the first assumption, we do not see that reason, if left to itself, would declare this to be impossible or certainly false.*"

Three views of reincarnation

Perhaps that heavy nineteenth century prose should be re-stated, though I did want to give you the Cardinal's exact words so you would know I was not putting a forced interpretation on them. What the Cardinal indicates is this: there are three possible beliefs about reincarnation:

1. that there is an immortal soul which goes from birth to birth until it attains salvation, which ends the rebirth process,

2. that the immortal soul is reborn eternally with no ending of rebirth, and

3. that there is no immortal soul, but only a kind of force or energy which keeps creating a chain of rebirths. In *A Manual of Modern Scholastic Philosophy*, Cardinal Mercier again enumerates the three views on reincarnation and this time states that the first view *"cannot be shown either to be impossible or even to be false"* (I, 326).

A public teaching?

But what about reincarnation as a public teaching? Being a persecuted religion for three centuries, the Church barely salvaged the Holy Scriptures from the ravages of her persecutors. Many books referred to by early writers as being widely used by the Church have vanished. Even the book of Enoch, quoted by Saint Jude in his epistle (v. 14), is no more; nor is the book of Jasher, mentioned in Joshua (10:13) and Second Samuel (1:18).

A Jewish belief

Reincarnation is commonly represented in the West as being an exclusively Hindu or Buddhist belief, but it is not. Reincarnation is a tenet of orthodox Judaism, wherein it is called *gilgul* or *ha'atakah*, and was so at the time of Jesus, and automatically passed over into Christian theology.

Philo Judaeus

The Jewish philosopher, Philo Judaeus, whose lifespan included that of Jesus, wrote in detail about reincarnation as a normal belief, but a brief quote should suffice:

> "The air is full of souls; those who are nearest to earth descending to be tied to mortal bodies return to other bodies, desiring to live in them" (*De Somniis* I:22). These words, which speak of souls returning to many earthly births from their desire to do so, are reminiscent of Solomon's words about his own ancient, cosmic past: "The Lord possessed me in the beginning of his way, before his works of old.... from the beginning, or ever the earth was....Then I was by him, as one brought up with him: and I was daily his delight, rejoicing always before him; rejoicing in the habitable part of his earth; and my delights were with the sons of men" (Proverbs 8:22, 23, 30, 31).

Josephus

The Jewish historian Flavius Josephus, nearly a contemporary of Jesus, recorded that both the Essenes and the Pharisees believed in rebirth (*not* in the resurrection of the physical body as is presently thought). The Pharisees, he tells us,

> "say that all the souls are incorruptible, but the souls of good men only, are removed into other bodies, but the

souls of bad men are subject to punishments lasting for ages."

That is, the good quickly reincarnate to work out their destined return to God, whereas the wicked undergo great sufferings in the other world, only getting the chance to return to the earth for further spiritual hope after the lapse of ages. He himself in a speech to some Jewish soldiers, said:

> "Do ye not remember that all pure spirits when they depart out of this life obtain a most holy place in heaven, from whence in the revolution of ages, they are again sent into pure bodies?" (*Jewish War*, Book 3, chapter 8, no. 5).

Note that he says: "Do ye not *remember*?" indicating that they had been taught reincarnation previously.

Solomon and Job speak

The above words of Josephus regarding the righteous spirits being sent into pure bodies after periods in heaven are an echo of further words of Solomon:

> "For I was a witty [wise] child, and had a good spirit. Yea rather, being good, I came into a body undefiled" (Wisdom 8:19, 20).

And Job had said:

"Naked came I out of my mother's womb, and naked *shall I return thither*" (Job 1:21).

Later on, Job expressed his conviction that he would be reborn on earth to behold the days of the Messiah.

"For I know that my redeemer liveth, and that he shall stand at the latter day upon the earth: and though after my skin, worms destroy this body, yet in my flesh shall I see God: Whom I shall see for myself, and mine eyes shall behold, and not another" (Job 19:25-27).

Although these words are commonly interpreted as referring to the end of the world and the resurrection of the physical body, an examination of the context of these words will show otherwise.

Rabbi Simeon ben Jochai

Rabbi Simeon ben Jochai, a contemporary of the Apostles, wrote:

"All souls are subject to the trials of transmigrations; and men do not know the designs of the Most High with regard to them;...They do not know how many transformations and mysterious trials they must undergo; how many souls and spirits come to this world without returning to the palace of the divine king."

These words, especially the reference about reincarnating souls not returning to "the palace of the divine king" are echoed in the Revelation of Saint John wherein Jesus says:

> "Him that overcometh will I make a pillar in the temple of my God, *and he shall go no more out*" (Revelation 3:12).

But Rabbi Simeon continues:

> "The souls must reenter the absolute substance whence they have emerged. But to accomplish this end they must develop all the perfections, the germ of which is planted in them; and if they have not fulfilled this condition during one life, they must commence another, a third, and so forth, until they have acquired the condition which fits them for reunion with God" (*Zohar*, vol. II, fol. 99, *et seq.*).

Once again, these words regarding a series of successive births for the purpose of attaining spiritual perfection are not just his own, but tie in with the inspired words of the book of Job:

> "Lo, all these things worketh God *oftentimes* with man, *to bring back his soul from the pit*, to be enlightened with the light of the living" (Job 33:29, 30).

"Fathers" and "Sons"

Also in keeping with the above are the symbolic words

spoken by God himself–words which, when misunderstood, have caused many to call them unjust:

> "The Lord is longsuffering, and of great mercy, forgiving iniquity and transgression, and by no means clearing the guilty, *visiting the iniquity of the fathers upon the children unto the third and fourth generation*" (Numbers 14:18).

In the most basic meaning, a "father" is a physical body which engenders other bodies. Thus, according to the mystical interpretation, "fathers" means our previous lives and bodies, the failures of which necessitate our being reborn in further bodies, which thereby are the "children" of those prior bodies. For they are engendered by the necessity for the workings of divine justice, which visits on these subsequent body "children" the iniquities of the original, "father" bodies. The prophet Ezekiel spoke of this phenomenon in this way:

> "The fathers have eaten sour grapes, and the children's teeth are set on edge" (Ezekiel 18:2).

We will consider the "how" of this later on in the explanation which Saint Paul gives in the New Testament.

This verse also gives a right perspective on karma and rebirth. *They are never intended as punishment.* We are plainly told that

> "the Lord is longsuffering, and of great mercy, *forgiving* iniquity and transgression."

Therefore there can be no question of God being angry or holding a grudge against us for any actions, however negative. Rather, as a loving and merciful Father he "forgives" us without our even asking for it. But there is a law whose execution is necessary for our spiritual development: the law of karma and rebirth. And we are not exempted (cleared) from its fulfillment, for that would not be mercy or forgiveness but harmful indulgence. The abrogation of a law that benefits us would be detrimental to us. God loves us too much for that.

Rabbi Manaseh ben Israel

Another witness to the stand of orthodox Judaism is the great Rabbi Manaseh ben Israel, who in the seventeenth century single-handedly obtained the repeal of the banning of Jews from England. In his book, *Nishmath Hayem*, he writes:

"The belief of the doctrine of the transmigration of souls is a firm and infallible dogma accepted by the whole assemblage of our church with one accord, so that there is none to be found who would dare to deny it.…Indeed, there are a great number of sages in Israel who hold firm to this doctrine so that they made it a dogma, a fundamental point of our religion. We are therefore in duty bound to obey and accept this dogma with acclamation…as the truth of it has been demonstrated by the *Zohar*, and all books of the Kabalists."

A Jewish prayer

Today, after a private recitation of the Song of Songs, an orthodox Jew recites the following in a prayer:

"...May we attain to that place from which all spirits and souls have come forth, and may we be credited with having fulfilled all that we have been charged to accomplish, *whether in this incarnation or in another incarnation,* and to be among those who ascend and merit the world to come together with the other saints and righteous...." (*Siddur Tikun Meir,* Hebrew Publishing Company, 1935).

Elijah...reincarnated!

Right away, in the New Testament, we encounter the subject of reincarnation. The Apostles believed that Jesus was the Messiah, but they had one doubt. In the book of Malachi there was the prophecy:

"Behold, I will send you Elijah the prophet before the coming of the great and dreadful day of the Lord" (Malachi 4:5).

If Jesus was the Messiah, Elijah should have preceded him. So

"his disciples asked him, saying, Why then say the scribes that Elias [Elijah] must first come? And Jesus answered and said unto them,...I say unto you, that Elias is come already, and they knew him not, but have done unto him whatsoever they listed....Then the disciples understood that he spake unto them of John the Baptist" (Matthew 17:10, 12, 13).

Previously, speaking to a crowd about John the Baptist, Jesus told them:

"This is he, of whom it is written, Behold, I send my messenger before thy face, which shall prepare thy way before thee....And if ye will receive it, this is Elias, which was for to come" (Matthew 11:10, 14).

Words could hardly be clearer, yet how many Christians today "are willing to receive it"? And they are the words of Jesus himself. As the modern philosopher-writer Robert Graves has commented about this passage:

"No honest theologian can therefore deny that his acceptance of Jesus as Christ [Messiah] logically binds every Christian to a belief in reincarnation—in Elijah's case, at least."

The common belief of the people

That the Jewish people believed in reincarnation is shown by the following interchange between Jesus and his disciples.

"When Jesus came into the coasts of Caesarea Philippi, he asked his disciples, saying, Whom do men say that I the Son of man am? And they said, Some say that thou art John the Baptist: some, Elias; and others, Jeremias, or one of the prophets" (Matthew 16:13, 14).

Some believed that John the Baptist had secretly escaped from prison and was preaching under an alias. But many more believed that one of the ancient prophets had been reborn as Jesus. This was because belief in reincarnation was the norm at that time. And nowhere in the Scriptures is it said that the Jews were in doctrinal error at the time of Jesus, or that he came to free them from false beliefs–he himself saying that he had only come to *fulfil* (Matthew 5:17).

Belief of the Apostles

The Apostles also believed in reincarnation, for:

"As Jesus passed by, he saw a man which was blind from his birth. And his disciples asked him, saying, Master, who did sin, this man, or his parents, that he was born blind? Jesus answered, Neither hath this man sinned, nor his parents: but that the works of God should be made manifest in him" (John 9:1-3).

Jesus would certainly have rebuked the Apostles for wrong belief if reincarnation was not true. Although the man's blindness was for the glory of God, the Lord said, "neither this man nor his parents sinned," implying that the man had certainly existed–and been capable of sinning–before his birth in which he was blind.

Non-belief in reincarnation rebuked by Jesus

When the Pharisee, Nicodemus, expressed his doubts as to a man being able to enter the womb and be born again, physically, saying:

"How can a man be born when he is old? can he enter the second time into his mother's womb, and be born?"

Jesus reproved him, saying:

"Art thou a master [teacher] of Israel, and knowest not these things?…If I have told you earthly things [about physical rebirth], and ye believe not, how shall ye believe, if I tell you of heavenly things [about the spiritual rebirth]?" (John 3:4, 10, 12).

especially when every educated Jew was familiar with the already-cited words of Job: "

Naked came I out of my mother's womb, and naked *shall I return thither*" (Job 1:21).

Moreover, every Jew had heard these words of Moses scores of times:

"Even from everlasting to everlasting, Thou art God. *Thou turnest man to destruction; and sayest, Return, ye children of men.…* Thou carriest them away like a flood; they are as a sleep: *in the morning they are like grass* which groweth up [again].…in the evening it is [again] cut down" (Psalm 90:2, 3, 5, 6).

This same idea was also to be found in the prayer of Tobit:

"Blessed be God that liveth for ever, and blessed be his kingdom. For he doth scourge, and hath mercy: *he leadeth down to hell* [hades], *and bringeth up again:* neither is there any that can avoid his hand" (Tobit 13:1, 2).

Also familiar would have been the direct reference to reincarnation in Ecclesiasticus:

"Woe be unto you, ungodly men, which have forsaken the law of the most high God! *For when you are born, you shall be born to a curse:* and when you die, a curse shall be your portion. All that are of the earth shall return to the earth again: so the ungodly shall go from a curse to destruction" (Ecclesiasticus 41:9, 10).

God's law behind reincarnation

But why? Saint Paul tells us:

"Be not deceived; God is not mocked: for *whatsoever a man soweth, that shall he also reap*" (Galatians 6:7).

In other words, if we lie, we shall be lied to; if we steal, we shall be stolen from; if we cheat, we shall be cheated; if we injure, we shall be injured; if we kill, we shall be killed. Is this law inexorable? In the verse from Numbers, previously quoted, it is flatly stated that the Lord by no means clears the guilty. This supports Saint Paul's contention that "God is not mocked."

This principle is not new to either of the Testaments, for when Noah had come forth from the Ark, God enunciated the law:

"Surely your blood of your lives will I require; at the hand of every beast I will require it, and at the hand of man.… Whoso sheddeth man's blood, by man shall his blood be shed" (Genesis 9:5, 6).

Notice that this is not a social law, such as those given to Moses. Noah is not being instructed to take the life of murderers; the Lord says, "*I will require it.*" Yet, how many murderers go undetected and unpunished? Think of the murderers that die natural deaths–even in prisons. Yet God, Who "is not mocked" has said that their life shall be taken by man. And this is in keeping with the next verse in Saint Paul's Galatians exposition: "For he that soweth to his flesh shall of the flesh reap"—that is, we shall reap *in our bodies* exactly what we sow in our bodies. And if we die before so doing? *Rebirth is the law.*

What about the objection that Saint Paul also wrote:

> "It is appointed unto men once to die, but after this the judgment" (Hebrews 9:27)?

Nothing, except Saint Paul's meaning:

> "Wherefore, as by one man sin entered into the world, and death by sin; and so death passed upon all men" (Romans 5:12).

Adam's transgression pronounced the death sentence upon all humanity. And, indeed, after each death we are judged to determine where we shall go in the astral world and when and where we shall return to earth in our next birth. It is interesting that the twentieth-century stigmatic, Teresa Neuman, saw that after death the departed soul was judged right here, some passing onward and others remaining in in the earth's astral atmosphere, obviously to await rebirth.

Jewish writings from the time of Jesus and the Apostles

Here are some quotations from Jewish writings that would have been studied by Saint Paul (See Acts 22:3; and 26:4, 5) and known to Jesus and the Twelve.

"Most souls being at present in the state of transmigrations, God requites a man now for what his soul merited in a bypast time in another body, by having broken some of the 613 precepts....He who neglects to observe any of the 613 precepts, such as were possible for him to observe, is doomed to undergo transmigration once or more than once till he has actually observed all he had neglected to do in a former state of being"(*Kitzur Sh'lu*, p. 6, col. I and II).

"The sages of truth remark that Adam contains the initial letters of Adam, David, and Messiah; for after Adam sinned his soul passed into David, and the latter having also sinned, it passed into the Messiah" (*Nishmath Chaim*, fol. 152, col. 2).

Regarding this, Gershom Scholem says in his book, *On the Mystical Shape of the Godhead*:

"The consonants in Adam's name are read as an acronym for the names of the three bearers of this one soul: Adam, David, Messiah. Kabbalistic literature is filled with discussions of this transmigration chain. At times this chain also includes Moses, the redeemer of Israel from its first Exile."

This latter statement is most significant in view of the fact that for many centuries on Good Friday during the exposition of Jesus Crucified the choir sings a hymn beginning:

"My people, what have I done to you? In what have I offended you, answer me?"

in which Jesus speaks to the people most explicitly of his life as Moses, contrasting it with his crucifixion.

"Becaue I led thee through the desert forty years: and fed thee with mann, and brought thee into a land exceedingly good, thou hast prepared a cross for thy Savior....I opened the sea before thee: and thou with a spear hast opened My side...I gave thee the water of salvation from the rock to drink: and thou hast given Me gall and vinegar...."

Scholem further says:

"The Kabbalists focus quite intensely on Adam's fall. Adam's transgression at the beginning of Creation is repaired by Moses, the lawgiver, by David, who established a throne for the Shekhinah, and will ultimately be perfected by the Messiah. The complementary relationship between the Fall and the Redemption, a notion first expressed by St. Paul and which also occupied the talmudic aggadah, is now given a Kabbalistic formulation in the doctrine of the transmigration of the Messiah's soul: the man who missed humanity's great chance in Paradise is the same one who will ultimately bring about its realization. The situation of Adam, Eve, and the serpent reappears in various guises throughout these transmigrations, each time needing to be overcome. An important Kabbalist of the late Middle Ages offered a highly dramatic retelling of the story of David, Bathsheba, and Uriah from this perspective. Paradoxically, David comes off a great deal better in this esoteric explanation than one might expect from the biblical tale: King David, of blessed memory, was a great sage and recognized transmigrations. When he saw Uriah the Hittite, he knew that he was the Serpent who had seduced Eve, and when he saw Bathsheba he knew that she was Eve, and he knew that he himself was Adam. Thus, he wished to take Bathsheba from Uriah, because she was [destined to be] David's mate....And the reason Nathan the prophet chastised him was because he hastened, and did not wait....For his haste caused him to go to her without performing tikkun (restoration), for he first needed to remove from her the contamination of the Serpent, and thereafter to go to her, and he did not do so. Therefore, his first son from Bathsheba died, for he was from the impurity of the Serpent, but from there on there was no Satan and no bad effect. In Tikkunei ha-Zohar (end of §61), Adam's reincarnation in Moses is clearly alluded to, albeit in the context of transferring Abel's sin onto Adam, and without any relation to the transmigrations of the Redeemer and of the Messiah: "'And Moses hid his face'–for he remembered what had happened to him before; he remembered his sin and covered himself in shame' similar to Adam's behavior after the sin."

In the book of Ezekiel we have proof that the Messiah was to be the reincarnation of David, for there we read:

"And I will set up one shepherd over them, and he shall feed them, *even my servant David*; he shall feed them, and he shall be their shepherd. And *David my servant* shall be king over them; and they all shall have one shepherd" (Ezekiel 34:23, 24).

Since Ezekiel lived four hundred years after David, his prophecy could only mean that David was going to reappear on the earth later as the Messiah. And he did.

But there are further ancient authorities for us to consider.

"Know thou that Cain's essential soul passed into Jethro, ... Samson the hero was possessed by the soul of Japhet, and Job by that of Terah" (*Yalkut Reubeni*, Nos. 9:24).

"Cain had stolen the twin sister of Abel, and thereafter his soul passed into Jethro. Moses was possessed by the soul of Abel, and therefore Jethro gave his daughter to Moses" (*Yalkut Chadash*, fol. 127, col. 3).

"If a man be niggardly either in a financial or a spiritual regard, giving nothing of his money to the poor or not imparting of his knowledge to the ignorant, he shall be punished by transmigration into a woman."

At the time this was written, women were prohibited to own property or to receive an education. Thus a man who did not use his possessions or knowledge to benefit others would be born in a body wherein he would be prevented from having them himself. And experiencing the bitterness of this deprivation, he would be sure to share his benefits in a future life, impelled by the subconscious memory of his soul.

Returning to the quotation:

"Know thou that Sarah, Hannah, the Shunammite [II Kings 4:8], and the widow of Zarepta were each in turn possessed by the soul of Eve....The soul of Rahab transmigrated into Heber the Kenite, and afterwards into Hannah; and this is the mystery of her words, 'I am a woman of a sorrowful spirit' (I Samuel 1:15), for there still lingered in her soul a sorrowful sense of inherited defilement....Eli possessed the soul of Jael, the wife of Heber the Kenite....Sometimes the souls of pious Jews pass by metempsychosis into Gentiles, in order that they may plead on behalf of Israel and treat them kindly" (*Yalkut Reubeni*, Nos. 1, 8, 61, 63).

Since Hannah, the mother of the prophet Samuel, was a reincarnation of Eve, it is appropriate to recall here her words:

"The Lord killeth, and maketh alive: he bringeth down to the grave, and bringeth up" (I Samuel 2:6).

That is, God causes man to die and then to live again; to go into the grave and then be born once more. Again we can recall the parallel words of Job already cited: "Naked came I out of my mother's womb, and naked shall I return thither."

A dramatic example

Certainly from the above we get the idea! Yet I cannot resist giving one more Biblical instance–bridging both the Old and the New Testaments–of how the human drama can be played out over the "acts" of several births on the stage of this world. (This example, by the way, was pointed out to me by Bess Hibarger, a Presbyterian Sunday School teacher of long standing and great popularity, who at least once a year devoted one Sunday to the subject of reincarnation.)

Ahab, the king of Israel, married Jezebel, who was a Gentile and an idolater. For these reasons, Elijah the prophet came to Ahab and challenged him, demanding that he rid himself of Jezebel. As could be expected, Jezebel decided that either Elijah or she had to go–and she preferred that it be Elijah. Though she had squadrons of soldiers searching for the prophet to kill him, he managed to elude them, and departed from this world still in hiding. Later, Jezebel died, but with the desire for the death of Elijah burning in her heart. Thus was the sowing; then came the reaping.

As Jesus said, Elijah was born again as John the Baptist. Ahab was reborn as Herod, and Jezebel as Herodias, the wife of Herod's brother. Herod broke the Law by marrying Herodias illegally, thus committing the double crime of adultery and incest. Just as in the previous lifetime, John came to Herod and demanded that he get rid of Herodias. Herod had respect for John, and so tried to simply ignore him. Finally, at the insistence of Herodias he imprisoned John, and ultimately

Herodias got John's head on a platter, fulfilling her desire of centuries.

Sowing and reaping in Gethsemane

In the closing hours of his life, Jesus also propounded the law of sowing and reaping.

> "One of them which were with Jesus stretched out his hand, and drew his sword, and struck a servant of the high priest's, and smote off his ear. Then said Jesus unto him, Put up again thy sword into his place: *for all they that take the sword shall perish with the sword*" (Matthew 26:51, 52).

Multitudes of people have lived by violence and themselves died quiet deaths–most of them unrepentant. Yet the Lord said they also would die by the sword. Has God then been "mocked"? Have they somehow escaped his law? Yes, they have, if there is no rebirth. But according to the foregoing Jewish authorities there indeed *is* rebirth, which is God's way of ensuring that "the wheels of divine justice may grind slowly, but they grind exceedingly fine."

Jesus reveals past lives

A further reference by Jesus to rebirth is found in his words to the great multitude shortly after he had miraculously fed them. Some of the crowd asked him:

"What sign showest thou then, that we may see, and believe thee? what dost thou work? Our fathers did eat manna in the desert; as it is written, He gave them bread from heaven to eat. Then Jesus said unto them, Verily verily, I say unto you, *Moses gave you not that bread from heaven*; but My Father giveth you the true bread from heaven" (John 6:30-32).

Notice that the Lord does not say "Moses gave *your fathers* not that bread from heaven," but instead: "Moses gave *you* not that bread from heaven," thereby indicating that those very persons who were challenging him had been with Moses in the desert. There, too, they had constantly challenged Moses and been unbelieving, and here with Jesus they continued the pattern. They were in fact the very persons to whom Moses had said:

"The Lord your God will raise up for *you* a Prophet like me from *your* midst, from *your* brethren. Him *you* shall hear" (Deuteronomy 18:15).

Again, see how Moses does not say "*your* children," but instead says "*you*," indicating that it would be those very ones to whom he was speaking that should see and hear the Messiah.

Reincarnation means responsibility

From all the foregoing we can draw the incontrovertible understanding that the individual soul, being endowed with free, creative will according to the divine image, must also shoulder the responsibility for that will–the responsibility being in the form of the irrevocable law:

"Whatsoever a man soweth, that shall he also reap."

The law is that we must receive back *whatever* we sow, not just a "suitable" punishment. This is reinforced by God's own words already cited when he told Noah,

"Whoever sheds man's blood, by man his blood shall be shed."

Retribution must be in the form of experiencing exactly what we have done to others–no substitute. For Jesus was not just putting forth a social directive when he said,

"All things whatsoever ye would that men should do to you, do ye even so to them" (Matthew 7:12).

He was simply restating the Law that whatever you do to others will in turn be done to you. And since "he that soweth to his flesh shall of the flesh reap," rebirth is an absolute necessity, to provide us the flesh in which to reap what we have sown.

Solomon's testimony

This is why Solomon said:

"The thing that hath been, *it is that which shall be*; and that which is done *is that which shall be done*: and there is *no new thing under the sun*. Is there any thing whereof it may be said, See, this is new? *it hath been already of old time, which was before us*" (Ecclesiastes 1:9, 10).

Solomon does not say "the same *type* of thing that hath been," but "*the thing*" itself is to reappear on the earth. From these words we learn several things:

1. It is the things and people of the past that will reappear on earth again as the *future* things and people.
2. It is the past actions which determine what the future actions will be, through the momentum of the law of sowing and reaping, or, more accurately, the past actions are *continued* as the future deeds. That is, the theft of today is the continuation of the theft committed in the past. To-day's murder is the "reaping" of a murder "sown" long ago.
3. *Nothing*, including the people, are here for the first time and "new" on the earth. None of us can claim that the earth life is something "new" for us. Rather, in the ages before this life it has already been known to us.

Rabbi Hillel speaks

Looking back momentarily to point (2), we find a most graphic stating of that principle in the *Daily Prayer Book*, edited by Philip Birnbaum (Hebrew Publishing Company, New York). In the second chapter of the section entitled: *Ethics of the Fathers*, the seventh section gives an incident from the life of Hillel, perhaps the greatest Rabbi in Jewish history, and a contemporary of Jesus:

> "He [Hillel] saw a skull floating on the surface of the water. He said to it: Because you drowned others, others have drowned you; and those who have drowned you shall themselves be drowned."

Is there an end to reincarnation?

Will there ever be an end to this? Yes, for

> "he that soweth to the *Spirit* shall of the *Spirit* reap life everlasting" (Galatians 6:8)

in those "everlasting habitations" (Luke 16:9), the "place for you" prepared by Jesus himself (John 14:2, 3), regarding which he promised:

> "Him that overcometh will I make a pillar in the temple of my God, and he shall go no more out" (Revelation 3:12), "neither can they die any more: for they are equal unto the angels; and are the children of God, being the children of the resurrection" (Luke 20:36), for "the last enemy that shall be destroyed is death" (I Corinthians 15:26),
> "for this corruptible must put on incorruption, and this mortal must put on immortality. So when this corruptible

shall have put on incorruption, and this mortal shall have put on immortality, then shall be brought to pass the saying that is written, Death is swallowed up in victory. O death, where is thy sting? O grave, where is thy victory?" (I Corinthians 15:53-55).

"Resurrection"–the end of reincarnation

A careful study of the relevant scriptures will reveal that the term "resurrection" indicates the state of freedom from rebirth and its corollary, death, and the ascension to Paradise from which Adam and Eve originally fell. In the Creed, we find the expression: "the resurrection *of the dead*," the "dead" being those subject to the law of sowing and reaping, of birth and death, who were helplessly caught in the wheels of that relentless Law until Jesus opened the way to freedom, to "resurrection" from the state of continual rebirth, and the return and restoration to Paradise.

"To him who overcomes I will give to eat from the tree of life, which is in the midst of the Paradise of God" (Revelation 2:7).

From Genesis to Revelation: reincarnation

In the Holy Scriptures, from Genesis to Revelation, the theme of reincarnation runs like a thread, binding together the two Testaments, and announcing the new Law of Grace and Freedom.

Early Christian writers

Now let us turn to early Christian writers–some of them Saints and Fathers of the Church–and see their testimony on the subject of rebirth. I will give the dates of their lives, so you can see in what era of the Church they lived.

Saint Clement of Alexandria (150-220)

"We were in being long before the foundation of the world; we existed in the eye of God, for it is our destiny to live in him....Not for the first time does he pity us in our wanderings, he pitied us from the very beginning.... Philolaus, the Pythagorean, taught that the soul was flung into the body as a punishment for the misdeeds it had committed, *and his opinion was confirmed by the most ancient of the prophets*" (*Stromata*, vol. 3, p. 433).

Origen (185-254)

"Is it not more in conformity with reason that every soul for certain mysterious reasons (I speak now according to the opinion of Pythagoras and Plato and Empedicles, whom Celsus frequently names) is introduced into a body, and introduced according to its deserts and former actions?...
"Is it not rational that souls should be introduced into bodies, in accordance with their merits and previous deeds, and that those who have used their bodies in doing the utmost

possible good should have a right to bodies endowed with qualities superior to the bodies of others?...

"The soul, which is immaterial and invisible in its nature, exists in no material place without having a body suited to the nature of that place. Accordingly, it at one time puts off one body, which was necessary before, but which is no longer adequate in its changed state, and it exchanges it for a second" (*Contra Celsum*).

"The soul has neither beginning nor end....Every soul comes into this world strengthened by the victories or weakened by the defeats of its previous life. Its place in this world as a vessel appointed to honor or dishonor is determined by its previous merits or demerits. Its work in this world determines its place in the world which is to follow this....

"The hope of freedom is entertained by the whole of creation–of being liberated from the corruption of slavery–when the sons of God, who either fell away or were scattered abroad, shall be gathered into one, and when they shall have fulfilled their duties in this world" (*De Prinicpiis*).

Origen is a controversial figure. The Emperor Justinian wanted him declared a heretic three hundred years after his death, and even had the acts of the Fifth Ecumenical Council falsified to accomplish this. Therefore, those who dislike Origen's theology bring forth the objection that he was not "orthodox." To refute this contention we need only turn to Saint Rufinus (345-410), whose holiness is recognized by both Eastern and Western churches. Not only did he insist that Origen was orthodox, he even made translations of Origen's works into Latin. In the preface to his translation of the just-quoted *De Principiis*, Saint Rufinus remarks that he has omitted anything that might at all be controversial. In other words, everything in his translation was acceptable to any Christian reader of his day, without exception. So let us look at three passages from this translation of Saint Rufinus which bears his attestation of orthodoxy:

(1) In Malachi and Romans are found the words: "Jacob I have loved, but Esau I have hated," which were spoken by God before their births; and also the ruling in Genesis that Esau should have to serve Jacob, though Jacob was younger. Like the words in Genesis about the visitation of the fathers' iniquities on the children, these words seem greatly unjust. But in the light of reincarnation they are seen differently. And here is what Origen had to say about it (please keep in mind that this and other quotations that follow are from the Latin translation of Saint Rufinus and therefore contain nothing that was offensive to the Christians of that day):

> "As, therefore, when the scriptures are examined with much diligence in regard to Esau and Jacob, it is found that there is 'no unrighteousness with God' (Romans 9:14) in its being said of them, before they were born or had done anything, in *this* life of course, that 'the elder should serve

the younger,' so also it is found that there is no unrighteousness in the fact that Jacob supplanted his brother even in the womb, provided we believe that *by reason of his merits in some previous life* Jacob had deserved to be loved by God to such an extent as to be worthy of being preferred to his brother" (*De Principiis*, II, 9, 7).

(2) "For perhaps, just as those who depart from this world by the common death of all, are distributed according to their deeds and merits, as a result of the judgment, some going to a place which is called the 'lower world,' others to 'Abraham's bosom' and to the various positions and dwelling-places in it; so the inhabitants of the region above, when they 'die' there, if one may so speak, descend from those upper places to this lower world.

"For the other lower world, to which are conveyed the souls of those who die on earth, is called by scripture, I believe on account of this distinction, 'the lower Hades,' as it says in the Psalms, 'And Thou hast delivered my soul from the lower Hades.' Each of those, therefore, who descend into the earth, is destined in accordance with his merits or with the position which he had held above to be born in a particular place or nation, or in a particular walk of life, or with particular infirmities, or to be the offspring of religious parents or the reverse, so that it happens occasionally that an Israelite falls among the Scythians and a poor Egyptian is conveyed to Judea....For in that case souls that are born on this earth of ours would either come from the lower world again to a higher place and assume a human body, in consequence of their desire for better things, or else would descend to us from better places. And so, too, those places which are above in the firmament may be occupied by some souls who have advanced from our seats to better things,..." (*De Principiis*, book 4, chapter 3).

(3) "The third order of rational creatures is composed of those spirits who are judged fit by God to replenish the human race. These are the souls of men, some of whom, in consequence of their progress, we see taken up into the order of angels, those, namely, who have been made 'sons of God' or 'sons of the resurrection' (Luke 20:36; Romans 8:14); or those who forsaking the darkness have loved the light and have been made 'sons of the light' (Luke 16:8); or those who, after winning every fight and being changed into 'men of peace,' become 'sons of peace' (Matthew 5:9; Luke 10:6) and 'sons of God' (John 1:12); or those who, by mortifying their members which are upon the earth (Colossians 3:5) and rising superior not only to their bodily nature but even to the wavering and fragile movements of the soul itself, have 'joined themselves to the Lord' (II Corinthians 6:17), being made wholly spiritual, so as to be always 'one spirit' with him, judging each individual thing in company with him, until they reach the point when they become perfect 'spiritual men' and 'judge all things,' because their mind is illuminated in all holiness through the word and wisdom of God, while they themselves are utterly incapable

of being judged by any man" (II Corinthians 11:15. *De Principiis*, I, 8, 4).

Saint Gregory of Nyssa (257-332)

"It is absolutely necessary that the soul should be healed and purified, and if this does not take place during its life on earth it must be accomplished in future lives" (*Great Catechism*).

In Saint Gregory's *Life* of his sister, Saint Macrina, whom he always referred to as "the teacher," he recorded that before her birth their mother, Saint Emmelia,

"fell asleep and seemed to be carrying in her hands that which was still in her womb. And some one in form and raiment more splendid than a human being appeared and addressed the child she was carrying by the name of Thecla, that Thecla, I mean, who is so famous among the virgins. After doing this and testifying to it three times, he departed from her sight."

Thus it was understood by her family that Saint Macrina was the reincarnation of the martyr, Saint Thecla, the greatest of Saint Paul's disciples. Because of this, all the family privately called her Thecla, though her public name was Macrina.

Arnobius (290)

"We die many times, and often do we rise from the dead" (*Adversus Gentes*).

Chalcidius (Third Century)

"Souls who have failed to unite themselves with God, are compelled by the law of destiny to begin a new kind of life, entirely different from their former, until they repent of their sins."

Nemesius, Bishop of Emesa (Fourth Century)

"Moses does not say that the soul was created at that moment at which it was put into the body, nor would it be reasonable to suppose it.... That the soul is not thus mortal and that man's destiny is not bounded by his present life is shown by the fact that the wisest of the Greeks believe in the transmigration of souls and that souls attain different grades according to the life they have lived" (*De Natura Hominis*).

Saint Jerome (340-420)

"The doctrine of transmigration has been secretly taught from ancient times to small numbers of people, as a traditional truth which was not to be divulged" (*Epistola ad Demetriadem*).

Saint Sulpitius Severus (363-420)

"As to Nero,…it was he who first began a persecution [of Christians]; and I am not sure but he will be the last also to carry it on, if, indeed, we admit, as many are inclined to believe, that he will yet appear immediately before the coming of Antichrist" (*Sacred History*, Chapter 28).

"[Nero is] to be sent forth again near the end of the world, in order that he may practice the mystery of iniquity" (*Sacred history*, Chapter 29).

This is most interesting. The thirteenth chapter of the book of Revelation is devoted to the subject of the Antichrist, or "Beast." The eighteenth verse says:

"Here is wisdom. Let him that hath understanding count the number of the beast: for it is the number of a man; and his number is Six hundred threescore and six."

The ancient commentaries on the book of Revelation are unanimous in saying that Nero is the "man of sin," the "beast." Students of those texts naturally assume that the early writers were wrong since Nero is long dead. But in the light of these words of Saint Sulpitius it is evident that they had a future incarnation of Nero in mind. So those commentaries are indirect evidence that the first Christians believed quite definitely in reincarnation.

Saint Augustine (354-430)

"The message of Plato, the purest and most luminous of all in philosophy, has at last scattered the darkness of error, and now shines forth mainly in Plotinus, a Platonist so like his master that one would think they lived together, or rather–since so long a period of time separates them–that Plato is born again in Plotinus" (*Contra Academicos*).

"Say, Lord, to me…say, did my infancy succeed another age of mine that died before it? Was it that which I spent within my mother's womb?…and what before that life again, O God my joy, was I anywhere or in any body?" (Confessions).

Synesius, Bishop of Ptolemais (370-430)

"Philosophy speaks of souls being prepared by a course of transmigrations….When first it comes down to earth, it [the soul] embarks on this animal spirit as on a boat, and through it is brought into contact with matter….The soul which did not quickly return to the heavenly region from which it was sent down to earth had to go through many lives of wandering" (*Treatise On Dreams*).

Saint Brigid of Kildare (525)

In his book *Round Ireland in Low Gear*, Eric Newby records that at this present day among the Catholics of Ireland there is a tradition that Saint Brigid in her previous life was the one who led the Virgin Mary to the place where she was purified at Bethlehem after the birth of Jesus.

Reincarnation a common belief

From these examples we can see that in the Apostolic Age and later, until Christianity was reshaped to suit the religio-political ideas of the Byzantine Emperors (who on occasion called themselves Vicars of Christ) and their political appointees whose "conversion" to Christianity was anything but sincere, reincarnation was so common as to be a truism among Christians.

Further evidence

In our inquiry it is the testimony of orthodox Judaism, ancient Christianity, and the Bible that is sufficient to answer our question: May a Christian believe in reincarnation?

Those who are interested in the witness of later Christian theologians and thinkers will find it most rewarding to look into the three books by Head and Cranston: *Reincarnation, An East-West Anthology; Reincarnation in World Thought;* and *Reincarnation: The Phoenix Fire Mystery.* There will be found statements of belief by such eminent Christians as Jacob Boehme, William Law, Henry Ward Beecher, Philips Brooks, Nicolas Berdyaev, Paul Tillich, Leslie Weatherhead, and Albert Schweitzer–plus many more.

Our conclusion

In summation: considering all of the foregoing material, we can positively conclude that Christians indeed *have* believed and *may* believe in reincarnation.

Perhaps even *must* believe.

A remarkable article on various scientific,
moral, and historical aspects of reincarnation
by Annie Besant (1847–1933), a renowned
speaker and writer, and president of the
Madras Theosophical society.

THE NECESSITY FOR REINCARNATION

by Annie Besant

First Published as Adyar Pamphlet No.113 in 1920

This question of Reincarnation is so large a one that in the title I have chosen I have limited the scope of our thought tonight. I do not pretend to deal with the whole of the doctrine, but with that special aspect of it: "The Necessity for Reincarnation."

The purpose of this consideration

There are many questions that will arise in the mind of the listener, many questions that in one brief lecture I cannot hope to answer: why we do not all remember the past; why we do not find, in looking back, clear mental illumination on the way in which our characters have grown, our thought-powers, our moral powers have developed. Many questions of that sort will arise, but if tonight I can succeed in showing you that there is at least a good case for Reincarnation as a rational explanation of life, of human progress, of human character; if I can show you that it enables us to understand many of the problems of life; if I can show you, as I shall try to do, that science demands it now in order to complete its theory of evolution; if I can show you that it is a necessity from the moral standpoint, if we would keep our belief in divine justice and divine love in facing many of the terrible facts of human life and of human pain; if I can show you that it is a necessity for human perfection; and then if, lastly, I can show you that, with all this pressing necessity to accept it, it is not a doctrine which belongs to Eastern religions alone; if I can show you that it is a doctrine that belongs to primitive Christianity as much as to other great religions of the world; if I can show you that in Christian antiquity it took its place unchallenged for five centuries among the doctrines taught by the great doctors and bishops of the Christian Church; if I can show you that it has never quite fallen out of Christian thought, that it has never quite lost its place in Christian literature, and that its revival today is the revival of a truth partially forgotten, and not an effort to graft into the Christian faith a doctrine from an alien creed; then perhaps, having shown the necessity, I may clear away something of the confusion in the mind of the ordinary Christian, which almost makes him shrink from considering the doctrine, and in this way may do all I hope to do, stimulate your own minds to think and to judge, stimulate your own powers of thought to accept or to reject as seems to you good.

For I do not hold that it is the duty of the lecturer to dogmatize, to lay down the law as to what another should think. I do not hold that it is the duty of the lecturer to do the thinking work, and then demand that the conclusion shall be accepted. The duty of the lecturer is only to put forth the truth as the truth is seen by him, leaving it to the individual reason and the individual conscience to reject or accept as seems to it good. That, then, is what I have to do, to put the case before you; you are the judges, not I.

Science and reincarnation

First, then, as to the scientific necessity for Reincarnation. Now, there are two great doctrines of evolution which may be said to divide the scientific world. One of them is falling rather into the background, the other coming more and more to the front. The first is the evolutionary teaching of Charles Darwin, the second, the later teaching of Weissmann. Now, these two doctrines are both important to us; both, in order to complete them, need this teaching of Reincarnation. For under both arise certain questions to which Reincarnation gives the only answer, certain problems which remain unsolved save in the light of this ancient and universal teaching.

I do not say that because the problems are unsolved by science, therefore this teaching is necessarily true; but I do say that when you find a doctrine put forward which explains problems, which explains that which science does not explain, answers difficulties that science does not answer, that then, that doctrine deserves at least a hearing in the minds of thoughtful men, in order that they may see whether there is not a possible explanation of the otherwise apparently inexplicable facts.

Darwin's theory

Take for a moment Charles Darwin's evolutionary teaching in the broadest possible light. Two great points come out as dealing with the progress of intelligence and of morality. First, the idea that qualities are transmitted from parent to offspring, and that by the accumulated force of that transmission intelligence and morality develop. As step after step is taken by human-kind, the results of the climbing are transmitted to the offspring, who, starting as it were from the platform built up by the past, are able to climb further in the present, and transmit enriched, to their posterity, the legacy that they receive. Along that line human progress seems possible and full of hope. Secondly, side by side with that stands the doctrine of conflict, of what is called "survival of the fittest;" of qualities which enable some to survive, and by the survival to hand down to their progeny those qualities that gave them an advantage in the struggle for existence.

Another perspective

Now those two chief points–transmission of quality from parent to offspring, survival of the fittest, in the struggle for existence–are two of the problems that are very, very difficult to deal with from the ordinary Darwinian standpoint. Transmission of qualities I will deal with at the same time as I speak of Weissmann; but on the second point, the question that we are obliged to ask the Darwinian with regard to the growth of the higher intelligence, and especially of moral qualities, is this: It is admitted that the qualities that are the most purely human–compassion, love, sympathy, the sacrifice of the strong for the protection of the weak, the willingness to give life for the benefit of others–these are the qualities that we recognize as human over against the qualities that we share with the brute. The more of these qualities show out in man, the more human is man considered to be, and so much is that recognized that the late

Prof. Huxley declared, in trying to deal with this problem, that you had to recognize that man, a fragment of the cosmos, set himself against the law of the cosmos; that he advanced by self-surrender, and not by the survival of the fittest; that he developed by self-sacrifice, and not by the trampling of the strong upon the weak, which was the law of growth in the lower kingdoms of nature.

And he asked the question: How is it that the fragment can set itself against the whole and evolve by a law which is against the law by which all the lower kingdoms developed? And he answered it in a tentative way: Is it because in man there is the same consciousness as that which underlies the universe? Whether he was prepared or not to answer the question in the affirmative we cannot say, but this remains from the mouth of the great preacher of evolution, that the law of progress for the man is the law of sacrifice and not the law of struggle.

But then, what does that mean? When you are face to face with the survival of the fittest, what does this mean? For those who sacrifice, themselves die out. How does mother-love arise and grow, even in the brute creation, among those we call the social animals, and even among the fiercest, the beasts of prey? How does that quality develop? How does it increase? Clearly we see that among the animals the mother sacrifices herself for her helpless offspring, conquering the law of self-preservation, the preservation of her own life, victorious over the fear of man which is interwoven in the nature of the brute that is wild. The mother bird, the mother animal, will sacrifice her own life in order to draw away her enemy, man, from the cave or the hiding-place where her young ones are hidden, mother-love triumphing over even the love of life. But she dies in the sacrifice. Those who show it most, perish–sacrifices to maternal affection; and if, as we must see when we look at it, the social virtues, the human virtues, tend to kill out their possessors and to leave the more selfish and more brutal alive, then how can you explain in man the growth of the spirit of self-sacrifice, how explain this continuing growth in the most divine qualities which incapacitate the man for the struggle of existence?

And Darwinism…

Now Darwinism does not really answer that question. Attempts are made to answer it. Those who have studied Darwinian writings know that the question is not fully faced, is rather evaded than answered. Reincarnation gives the answer that, in the continuing life, whether of the animal or of the man, that self-sacrifice stirs up on the side of character a new power, a new life, a compelling strength, which comes back over and over again to the world in ever higher and higher manifestations; that though the form of the mother perishes, the mother-soul survives, and comes back time after time; those who are such mother-souls are trained onward, first in the brute kingdom and then in the human kingdom, so that that which is gained by the soul at the sacrifice of the body comes back in the reincarnating soul to bless and to lift the world. The persistence of the soul it is that makes that growth in moral character possible.

Transmission of qualities

We come to the question of transmission of qualities that, as I said, leads us into the view of Weissmann. Weissmann has established two fundamental facts: first, the continuity of physical life–fairly clear to ordinary vision, but proved by him in a way that goes further than any scientific thought went before him–on the one side continuity of physical life, and we shall see that we need, to complete it, continuity of intellectual and moral life. And the reason we need it along the Weissmann line is his second fundamental fact. Weissmann declares–and ever more and more is that view being accepted–that mental and moral and other acquired qualities are not transmitted to offspring, that they can only be transmitted when they have worked themselves slowly and by degrees into the very fabric of the physical body of the people concerned.

Mental and moral qualities not being transmitted–and the evidence for this is becoming overwhelming–where will you have the reason for human progress, unless, side by side with the continuity of protoplasm, you have the continuity of an evolving, of a developing soul? Not only is that necessary, but along with this same theory, backed up as it is by facts of observation, we find that the higher the organism the greater the tendency towards sterility, or towards a very great limiting of the number of the offspring produced.

Genius–it is becoming almost a commonplace in science–genius is sterile, and by that it is meant that the genius does not tend in the first place largely to increase the number of the race, and secondly, that even where a genius has a child, the child does not show the qualities of the genius, but for the most part is commonplace, tending even to be below the average of the time. Now that is a subject of enormous importance for the future. For the genius of today ought to mark the normal level of hundreds of years hence. The genius of today, whether the genius of intellect or of virtue, the high-water mark of present human progress, should show the place to which the ocean will rise presently, as the generations go on. If he is only a mere sport of nature, if he is only the result of some fortunate accident, if he is only the outcome of some unknown cause, then he brings us no message of hope, no promise for the future; but if it be that in that individual genius you are to find a soul who by long experience has gathered the qualities with which he was this time born; if it be that, side by side with the continuity of protoplasm, there is also a continuity of soul, growing, developing, evolving, as forms grow, develop and evolve, ah! then the genius is only the forerunner of a greater humanity, and the lowest child of earth may hope in future to climb to the height of intelligence or of virtue on which he stands.

And this view of genius is strengthened by investigation; for we notice that genius is to be found along two special lines–that of the genius of pure intellect or virtue, and that of the artist that demands a peculiar co-operation of the body. The first asks little or nothing from physical heredity, but you cannot have the great genius in music unless you have with it a specialized body, a delicacy of nervous organization; a fineness of touch, a keenness of ear. These physical things are required in order that musical genius may show itself forth at its highest. There the co-operation of physical heredity is demanded, and what do you find when you study the stories of musical genius? That he is generally born in a musical family; that for two or three generations before the great genius, some amount of musical talent has been marked in the family in which he appears; and that when he, the genius, appears, then that musical talent dies out, and the family goes back into the ordinary run of average people. The family flowers in the genius; he does not hand on his genius to his posterity.

How reincarnation explains

Now those problems and puzzles of heredity find their rational explanation in the teaching of Reincarnation; for what is it? It is the teaching that breathed into the form is a portion of the life of God. Like a seed, a germ, the germinal spirit comes forth into the world of matter, with all divine possibilities hidden within it, as within the seed the possibilities of the plant that gave it birth are hidden; in that germinal spirit are all divine powers, that man may become perfect as his Father in heaven is perfect. But in order that that perfection may be attained, there must be growth, experience, evolution; in each life on earth experience must be gathered; in the long interval between death and rebirth the experience gathered on the earth is woven in the invisible worlds into the fabric of the soul; when that germinal spirit comes back to earth, it comes with this soul-clothing of qualities woven out of the experience gathered in its previous life on earth, and the innate ideas of the child are the result of the weaving–during the heavenly life– into quality of the experience of the earth-life that lies behind.

When that experience is transmuted into quality, then spirit and soul come back to earth, start on the platform already gained by experience and by struggle, and carry on the evolution with the advantage of the innate qualities which are the result of the previous life. During the new life more experience, more struggle, material for further growth; the weaving of that again into higher qualities during the renewed interval between death and rebirth. And so, on and on, rung after rung of the ladder of progress; at the bottom of that human ladder the lowest savage; at the top of that human ladder, the greatest saint and the noblest intellect, genius built up by slow degrees, built up by countless struggles, built up by failure as well as victory, by evil as well as good, the evils of the past the steps whereon man rises into virtue, so that even in the lowest criminal we see the promise of divinity. He, too, shall rise where the saint is standing, and in all the children of men God shall at last be seen. That is the theory of Reincarnation.

Now, let us see if it does not fit the facts from the scientific standpoint. We see now how the genius will have grown. He does not come suddenly into the world with nothing behind him, suddenly God-created. He comes with the qualities he has gradually developed by struggle in his past. We can understand, as we look at him, why the children of today, born of civilized parents, respond quickly to moral teaching, answer to moral appeal; and why a child of the savage, a young soul, a child-soul, cannot respond to those teachings, no matter how carefully you may try to instruct him. The answer of the children of the civilized man of today to the moral ideal, to moral precepts, is almost immediate. The child responds to it by nature; the child of the savage does not so. You cannot take the savage child and lift him to the point at which your own children are to be found whilst still in the nursery. They have not the power to respond.

But the moment you admit the continuing spirit, the moment you admit the weaving into quality of experiences, that in the character of the new-born child you can see the results of his past, then you begin to understand why man should have progressed, even though Weissmann be right when he says that acquired qualities are not transmitted; for those mental and moral qualities are not the gift of the parent, they are the hard-won spoils of victory of the individual soul; and each soul comes to his birth into the new body with the results of his past lives in his hand to work with in the present. Thus this theory fills up the gaps in the scientific one, answers the problems that science cannot answer, and more and more it appears, as we notice the lines of evolution of modern science, that this theory of Reincarnation is wanted in order to complete the theory and to make intelligible the progress of character and intelligence side by side with the evolution of the form.

Soul-age

Moreover, the marks of growth that we see among men are clear signs of a past, of difference of soul-age, if I may use the word. Wherever you go through nature, looking at things of the same kind, you find them at different stages of growth; and you constantly find in the more developed creature marks of the past up [from] which he has evolved. Now, this is not only true of bodies; it is equally true of the soul in man, for you see, when you look at man, all stages of intelligence, all stages of moral growth. At the present moment in this one country, in this one town, you could bring together thousands of men at different stages of evolution in intelligence and in moral capacity. How are they to be explained? I am not now thinking of the moral point, to which I shall come in a moment. How are they to be explained scientifically? Why these great differences? Or why even the small differences? If you say 'growth', you are on sound scientific ground, because everywhere in nature you see growth, differences of size, differences of development, and these are stages of the growth of the living creature.

Why only in intelligence and morality is this principle of growth to be thrown on one side, as explaining differences of state, and the principle–thrown out everywhere by science–the theory of sudden creation, of a sudden appearance without cause, without antecedents, without anything to explain it, be held to explain (if the word may be used) the differences in the growth of intelligence and of morality in different human beings? Moreover, you find in human intelligence marks of its past, similar to the marks of the past in human bodies; intelligence in anew body swiftly runs over its past evolution, as all careful observers of the unfolding of intelligence in the child know well.

Depravity

But that brings me to the moral question. I said that Reincarnation is a necessity morally, if we are to keep our belief in the divine justice and the divine love face-to-face with the facts of life. Now let me take two cases, the reality of which will be very plain to everyone of you. I choose extreme cases in order to make the illustration very clear. Go down into one of the worst slums of London. Children are born into those slums of vilest parentage; looked at from the point of view of physical heredity, looked at from the moral and intellectual status of father and mother. Now you can tell one of the children of whom I am thinking, a child-criminal, when you see it in the cradle; you know, as you look at that baby form, that that child is doomed to a life of misery and crime. You can tell it by the shape of the head, you can tell by the whole type of the features that that child is a criminal child. And it is true. They are the despair of the educator, as I know who have had to deal with them, as all know who are brought into touch with them. They will not respond to moral appeal, but only to fear, most brutalizing of instructors. There is no moral answer at all; there is no answer such as anyone of you would find from a child in your own nursery.

The child comes into the world with the criminal taint upon him. How is he brought up? He is brought up in that miserable surrounding that some of you may know, where the teachers of the child are blows and curses, where the child is taught to steal as you teach your child to be honest, where he is flogged for not lying, where vice is rewarded, where any attempt at right-doing is punished. That is the atmosphere in which he is brought up. He is taught to look upon society as his enemy, the law as his tyrant, the policeman as his foe–to have his hand turned against society. What is the inevitable result? That he falls into the hands of the law. The law nowadays tries to be more merciful than it was twenty or thirty years ago, and tries reform. But reform is only possible where there is something within the brain and heart to respond to it. And I am taking the case–there are only too many of them–where this power of response is not found. He goes on from one crime to another, from one imprisonment to another, gradually developing into that shame of our civilization–a habitual criminal. From one stage of vice to another he proceeds, none to help him, none to rescue him, none to uplift him, until at last, in some mad moment of despair, or drunkenness, or passion, he strikes an angry blow that takes a human life, and then human justice takes from him the life which has slain another, and he ends his miserable career in the quicklime of the prison-yard. His fault? He never had a chance. He came into the world a criminal; he has left it a criminal. That is his life's story.

Genius

Another child is born, and as you look on that child in the cradle you see the stamp of genius upon him from the birth hour; you see in the shape of head and type of feature the splendor of the human soul that resides within that baby form. He is born of noble parents, who surround him with all gentleness, and kindness, and tenderness. He is petted and caressed into nobility of living, as the other was beaten into crime. Every effort he makes is encouraged; he hears around him all words of cheer and inspiration where the other had naught but curses and derision. His splendid qualities grow and expand: he becomes greater and greater as year after year passes over his head. He is given the very best education the land can give; his countrymen salute his genius as the glory of their race. On, year after year, he goes, ever brighter and brighter, climbing higher and higher, until at last, amid a nation's sorrow, Westminster Abbey receives the remains of his mortal body, and his name shines, a star in history, which all men admire and revere. His merit? He was born into the world a genius.

From whence…

Who sent those two souls on their life's journeys? If you say that the criminal came newly into the world God-created, and the genius came also newly into the world God-created, ah!

then what becomes of the divine justice upon which the hopes of humanity must rest? For if the one could be made straight from his Creator's hands, why should the other be made? If the genius in intellect can be created, why then the idiot? If the saint can be created, why then the criminal?

Necessity of the answers

I know you may say: "These are not questions that we can answer." But it is these questions that drive hundreds of noble hearts into infidelity, into a skepticism which is really more reverent than belief. I speak of what I know. These are the things that made me an unbeliever for many, many years. It was human pain and, worse than human pain, human degradation—for human sin is worse than human misery—it was those facts that made me an unbeliever; for I preferred not to believe in God rather than to believe in a supreme injustice and the lack of love at the world's heart.

And these questions are not the questions of the thoughtless, the indifferent and the profligate; they are the questions of ripe intelligences and of noble hearts. And religion must find an answer to these questions if she is to keep the noblest of the children of men within her pale. There is one reason why I ask for discussion of this question, and why it seems to me that it is the religious teachers of the people who are most concerned in such problems of human life.

One life and many lives

Now look at this same thing still from the standpoint of

justice and of love. Some religious people believe that this one human life decides the whole course of the future. Others do not accept that view, but think that on the other side of the grave progress, or happiness for all, is possible. Now if progress be admitted, then the whole principle of Reincarnation is granted. For, whether it be in this or in other worlds, if progress be admitted as the law of life, the growth of the spirit and the soul is granted. But suppose, with the great majority in Christendom, that men believe either that this life decides the whole fate of the soul hereafter, or believe that though all will pass into bliss, this life is but one, one single life, then how very difficult to reconcile the facts with that. For a human soul is born into the world in a baby's body and dies in a few days. Another goes through a long life of sixty or seventy years. If the first idea be accepted, that this life decides the whole future, then it becomes very hard for the man who lives out his life to run the risk of eternal loss, from which the baby, by the mere fact of his early death, is secured. A terrible injustice that, when you come to think of it; because none would say that the child who dies a few hours old runs any risk of misery hereafter. Then why should he reap the fruit of bliss which may be forfeited by the older man in his struggles in the world in the course of his long life? This difference of the length of human life becomes inseparable from the question of justice, if you are going to admit only this one life. And if you say that, of what use is the life if the child, who has only had two or three hours of it, reaches the same everlastingness of bliss as the man who, through a life of struggle, has won virtue and triumphed over temptation?

Does it matter?

Does this life matter or not? That is the problem to be solved. If it does not matter, and the newborn babe dying finds eternal happiness, then it is very hard that so many should have to go through a life of pain and suffering and have nothing to show for it at the end. What avails that experience if this theory of life be true? And when the old man dies full of wisdom, full of the fruits of experience, full of tender sympathy and compassion, where are those fruits that he has won by life's experience to be utilized? In a life of ceaseless bliss? They are of no use in such a life. But this world has need of them. This world wants them. And if he can bring them back here to the service of humanity, after the growth on the other side has woven them into his very nature, ah! then that long life will indeed have its fruit in human service, and we can realize the value of the physical life as one of the factors in the universe. And if it be admitted that human life has its use on the other side, then what of the babe who is shut out from the one chance of valuable experience, and goes through everlastingness with a perpetual want, the want of that one human life which others have possessed?

"Be ye perfect"

And pass again to another question, which has always seemed to me even more important from the standpoint of the divine life–a life of degradation, the life of the drunkard, of the undeveloped human soul, who simply slouches through the world with his eyes down, with his mind unawake, with no power to appreciate the beauty of this wonderful world, and all the marvelous things that are to be found within its limits. Compare such a creature as that, whose life is nothing more than a few bodily sensations, a few passions, and an occasional crude thought–compare that, his only experience of human life, with the life of the cultured, thoughtful, well-developed intelligence, who takes joy in all beauty, in all that is gracious and fair in the world; and ask why one should have as his only experience of life that miserable crawling through the slime of earth, while the other, born, just as the first was born, with nothing behind him, is to soar into visions of beauty and delight, and find in his experience of the earth so much that makes it fun and beautiful and helpful?

The truer perspective

It is not fair, it is not right, if we all have but the one experience. How does Reincarnation deal with that? It tells us that out from the bosom of the eternal Father come all these germinal spirits that He sends into the world of matter for their growth and development; that all begin ignorant, helpless; that all gradually grow upwards, developing their inherent powers; that man is born into the world to become perfect. Has it ever struck you to ask what mean those wondrous words of the Christ: "Be ye therefore perfect, as your Father in heaven is perfect"? Think how magnificent that ideal. And how is it to be done? Why even we, who, according to this teaching of Reincarnation, have climbed so high from our earliest beginnings in this spirit life, can we say, with our weaknesses and our follies, with the limitations of our knowledge and of our power, that in this one life, even starting with all the advantages we have, we can become perfect as God in heaven is perfect? And yet nothing less than that is man's destiny; that, and nothing less than that, is the word of the Christ to His disciples. Surely He who is called "The Truth" would not have given a command which cannot be fulfilled.

But we have this divine perfection within us, as within the seed is the power of the tree. And we need but time for the fulfilling of the command, for the growth into the splendor of the Image in which we are made. So that from that standpoint also this seems to be necessary. You may say: "Yes, in other worlds;" but, then, why? What is the sense of sending people at every stage of growth into this one particular world? Where did the higher ones earn their powers? In other worlds before birth? If so, why come for one lesson into this world, and then go on into other worlds again? For all the varieties are here, lowest and highest, and every step between. And if you admit growth on the other side, then you must explain the differences of growth in this world–why one is dowered with so much more than another.

The school of life

Is it not more likely, more reasonable, more in accordance with all we know of nature, that this world is a school into which come souls, beginning in the infant class, going on stage after stage, which is life after life, until they reach the highest class in the school, and then going on in the other worlds, where other lessons are to be learned, a vast progress of unending evolution? But in this world certain classes have to be passed through which cannot be passed through in the limits of a single life. So that from that standpoint also Reincarnation seems to be a necessity, to say nothing of the glory and the inspiration that it gives to human life. For if I know, in this life of mine, that every effort I am making, every aspiration in which I lift my heart to God, every hope that I strive to realize, every service that imperfectly I try to do, is the seed of a harvest that shall have its reaping, is the building of a faculty that hereafter I may use in divine and human service; if I know that, however weak, however failing, however ignorant, everything that I learn is mine for everlasting, and that I shall come back again and again until all life's lessons are learned; ah! then I shall not break my heart because I am still ignorant, because I am still foolish, because I am still sinful; I shall know that although I am weak today I shall be strong tomorrow, and that there is not one height reached by the highest saint which shall not also be mine in time to come, who am climbing the same ladder that he has climbed so long.

New hope

There is the hope of evolution brought into the life of the individual; there the glory that Reincarnation sheds on human life; for when I now see the downcast, the miserable, the lowest of human kind, I can feel: You are only my younger brother, a baby in the school of life, where I have been for a longer period than you; the same God lives in you that lives in me; and I have for him the tenderness, the compassion, that the elder brother feels for the baby struggling on the floor. It is with no hatred, no contempt, no derision, that I regard him, but with the recognition of a common life which will be unfolded in him tomorrow, as I in years gone by struggled also where he struggles now. There is the secret for the uplifting of the degraded, which it seems to me that nothing else can give; for if they do not catch this idea, there is a sense of injustice, of unfairness, of being flung into a world into which they did not ask to come, into misery and into degradation. But if it is only the beginning of the experience of the divine life within them, the learning of the alphabet of life, then there is no feeling of despair nor of anger, but perfect justice as well as perfect love is at the heart of the world. For there is only one explanation, it seems to me, of love side by side with human misery, and it is that this education is necessary for the unfolding of the divine powers in man. If it is not necessary, it is not born of love. And if it be necessary, then it cannot be escaped by any; all must go through it or else remain forever imperfect, because they have not had that experience in human life.

Reincarnation in Christian teaching

Pass from the view of the necessity, and let us ask whether this, which seems so necessary, is a doctrine which does not belong to Christendom as much as to any other people, to any other faith. Now every student knows that this doctrine was common amongst the Jews. You may read in their books that it was the common faith of the time. You can see it in the questions that in the Gospels are sometimes put to the disciples and to the Christ. Remember the words spoken, by the Christ Himself to the disciples when they questioned Him of John the Baptist: "If you can receive it, this is Elijah." Remember His answer when they brought to Him the challenge of the people outside "How say the scribes that Elijah must first come?" His answer was: "He has come already; and they understood that He spoke to them of John the Baptist." This is simply one case showing the familiarity of the idea among the Jews, just as you may find it in the writings I refer to, that they said that all imperfect souls had to return to the earth. Then take, still within the limits of the Gospels themselves, that remarkable statement about the man born blind. "Which did sin, this man or his parents, that he was born blind?" Ante-natal sin. Now the answer that was given: "Neither did this man sin nor his parents that he was born blind," and another reason being given, is very significant. For if the knowledge of the Christ had been the same as the ordinary belief nowadays, that ante-natal sin is impossible, the only answer would have been: "Why ask me the foolish question whether a man is born blind because of his sin? How could he sin before birth?" A different reason was given for the blindness, but not a natural rebuke of the folly which ascribed a defect at birth to the sin of the individual who was born.

In early Christianity

Come away from those authoritative records of Christianity to the writings and teachings of those who lived in the early centuries after Christ, and see how often in the writings of the great Fathers of the Church this doctrine of the pre-existence of the soul is taught. One of the plainest teachings of it is found in the writings of that noblest of the Fathers, Origen. He lays it down distinctly that each person born into the world receives a body according to his deserts and his former actions; a very, very clear statement. And Origen, remember, was one of the grandest minds of which the early Church could boast, one of the noblest and purest characters, and he taught that doctrine definitely and clearly. Take other great bishops, and you will find them speaking along the same line; for five-and-a-half centuries after the death of Christ that was a current doctrine of the Christian Church. And when, in the middle of the sixth century, it was condemned by a council, it was not condemned as a general doctrine, but only in the form in which Origen had put it, so that you have absolutely no Christian authority against it. The Roman Catholic may object to the form into which Origen threw it, and say that that form was condemned by a council of the Church, but he cannot say that the whole doctrine of Reincarnation was condemned, for there is no such condemnation of the doctrine known in Christian history. On the other hand, you have it taught over and over again by the men who received the original deposit of the Faith. And it never quite disappeared. Granted that it disappeared from the authorized, the official, teachings of the Church, it survived in many of the so-called heretical bodies. The Albigenses taught it. Many other bodies, through the Middle Ages and onwards, claimed a truer tradition than that of the Roman Church, and carried this doctrine on as part of the primitive tradition.

And when you come down through the various Christian writers, how often does this doctrine come to the front, especially amongst the philosophers and poets–the poets because of their intuitions; the philosophers because, as Hume said, the only doctrine of the immortality of the soul at which the philosopher can look is a doctrine that affirms its pre-existence. And that necessarily; for once the philosopher allows it is necessary for the existence of a soul that it should be provided with a human body at birth, there follows the probability that when death strikes away that body, the soul will no longer be able to exist. And one of the roots of modern skepticism lies in this most illogical doctrine–that a soul which is to last for ever after death did not exist for ever before birth.

In modern Christianity

Then later, you find it appearing in a very interesting manner in the Church of England. I came across, some three years ago, a pamphlet written by a clergymen of the Church of England of the seventeenth century, in which he laid it down as an essential doctrine of Christianity that the soul existed before birth, and he quoted in that pamphlet a number of other pamphlets written about the same time, putting forward the same teaching, giving quotations from them, as well as tracing it back through the early Fathers and through the great Churches of Christendom. And he, though putting forward that view, apparently had no condemnation from his Bishop, nor from anyone who objected to his view as being really Christian teachings. Take the German philosophers; you find it among them necessarily.

Take Goethe, one of those great intuitional minds who see the truth that lies behind the appearance of things. Or have you forgotten that most Christian of poets, Wordsworth, and his declaration, long before the Theosophical Society came to disturb people's minds in this country?

> Our birth is but a sleep and a forgetting
>   The soul that rises with us, our life's star,
> Hath had elsewhere its setting,
>   And cometh from afar.
> Not in entire forgetfulness
>   And not in utter nakedness
> But trailing clouds of glory do we come
>   From God who is our home.

There you have his view: "Hath had elsewhere its setting." Poet after poet teaches the same, poet after poet who by the light of genius sees through the veil of matter and realizes by the poetic intuition the truth about the human soul.

The overview

Now surely if we find this doctrine taught by the early Fathers, strongly hinted at, if nothing more–I should say asserted–by the Christ, existing in Christendom through its whole history, even though thrown aside by the official Church, reappearing again in England in the very bosom of the English Church in the seventeenth century, reaffirmed by English poets and German philosophers, is it not better to look at it as a part of the great heritage of Christendom rather than as an alien doctrine coming from other religions? It is perfectly true, of course, that every great religion of the past has taught this doctrine. It is true you find it in the Book of the Dead; that you find it in Chaldea; that you find it in the ancient teachings in China; that you find in all the Indian scriptures, and in the Buddhist scriptures; that you find it in Greece and in Rome. But it is not because of that that I am putting it forward here, in an audience gathered in a Christian land.

Reincarnation belongs to Christianity

I say to you, it is yours as much as theirs, and if you accept the doctrine of Reincarnation, do not accept it as an alien doctrine that comes from some other faith; take it as part of the great Christian revelation; take it as part of the great Christian teaching. Admit that it fell out of sight for a while under the blackness of ignorance that swept over Europe. Admit that it dropped below the surface, in times when men were not thinking of these great problems that face you today. But as you value the work that this Faith is to do in the West, the one religion which is possible in the West, for to the West it was given, do not, as you prize that Faith, put aside as alien, as heretical, a doctrine which is coming back into the Christian Church by some of its best thinkers, by some of its best teachers. Clergyman after clergyman in the Church of England has accepted it, and is beginning to teach it. Writer after writer is seeing in this the safety of Christianity from the shafts of skepticism arising from the conscience as well as from intellect. And I put it to you today for your consideration–not for your acceptance, because the belief that can be gained by listening to one brief lecture would be worthless as an intellectual conviction and useless in its bearing upon life–I ask you to think, to consider, to clear away the prejudice which looks on it as unchristian and as alien, to recognize that, if it be true, then inevitably it is part of the truth of Christianity, and that history will justify you in that statement, showing it to be part of the Faith once delivered to the Saints.

Reincarnation, doctrine of hope and strength

Friends, if I speak to you on this tonight, it is because I know what the doctrine has of hope, of strength, of encouragement, in the face of the difficulties in the world. I know what it means for the heart-broken, who fall in despair before the puzzles of life, to have the light thrown upon it which makes life intelligible; for the misery of intellectual unrest is one of the worst miseries that we face in the modern world. To be able to understand what we are, to be able to understand whence we have come and whither we are going, to see all through the world one law as there is one life, to realize that there is no partiality, no injustice, no unfair treatment of one human soul, no unfair treatment of one human life; that all are growing; that all are evolving; that our elders are only elders and not different in kind from ourselves;

that the youngest shall be as the oldest; that man has within him the developing spirit of his Father and shall therefore be perfect as God is perfect; that is the hope–nay, not the hope, the certainty–that this doctrine gives to the human soul. And when we have grasped it we can face the miseries, the sorrows, the despairs of life, and know that in the end, looking back upon this sorrowful world, we shall say: "It was from God, it came from God, and to God it returns."

Did you enjoy reading
May a Christian Believe in Reincarnation?
Please take a moment and
give this book a review on
Amazon.com.

About the Author

Abbot George Burke (Swami Nirmalananda Giri) is the founder and director of the Light of the Spirit Monastery (Atma Jyoti Ashram) in Cedar Crest, New Mexico, USA.

In his many pilgrimages to India, he had the opportunity of meeting some of India's greatest spiritual figures, including Swami Sivananda of Rishikesh and Anandamayi Ma. During his first trip to India he was made a member of the ancient Swami Order by Swami Vidyananda Giri, a direct disciple of Paramhansa Yogananda, who had himself been given sannyas by the Shankaracharya of Puri, Jagadguru Bharati Krishna Tirtha.

In the United States he also encountered various Christian saints, including Saint John Maximovich of San Francisco and Saint Philaret Voznesensky of New York. He was ordained in the Liberal Catholic Church (International) to the priesthood on January 25, 1974, and consecrated a bishop on August 23, 1975.

For many years Abbot George has researched the identity of Jesus Christ and his teachings with India and Sanatana Dharma, including Yoga. It is his conclusion that Jesus lived in India for most of his life, and was a yogi and Sanatana Dharma missionary to the West. After his resurrection he returned to India and lived the rest of his life in the Himalayas.

He has written extensively on these and other topics, many of which are posted at OCOY.org.

MORE FROM LIGHT OF THE SPIRIT PRESS

By Abbot George Burke (Swami Nirmalananda Giri)

Om Yoga Meditation: Its Theory and Practice

❧

**The Christ of India:
The Story of St. Thomas Christianity**

❧

**The Gospel of Thomas for Awakening: A Commentary on
Jesus' Sayings as Recorded by the Apostle Thomas**

❧

**A Brief Sanskrit Glossary: A Spiritual Student's Guide to
Essential Sanskrit Terms**

❧

**The Dhammapada for Awakening: A Commentary on
Buddha's Practical Wisdom**

More of Abbot George Burke's writings can be found at the website of Light of the Spirit Monastery, OCOY.org.

You will find many articles on Original Christianity and Original Yoga, including *Esoteric Christian Beliefs*, and *Robe of Light*, a Christian Cosmology. *The Word That is God* is an in-depth collection of citations from the scriptures and spiritual masters on Om. *How to Be a Yogi* is a practical guide for anyone seriously interested in living the Yoga Life.

And you will also discover many practical articles on leading an effective spiritual life, including *Foundations of Yoga* and *Spiritual Benefits of a Vegetarian Diet*, as well as in-depth commentaries on these spiritual classics:

- the Bhagavad Gita,
- the Upanishads,
- the Tao Teh King
- the Aquarian Gospel of Jesus the Christ.

Recently added are a series of podcasts by Abbot George on meditation, the Yoga Life, and remarkable spiritual people he has met in India and elsewhere.

Visit OCOY.org today.

Made in the USA
Las Vegas, NV
03 February 2023

66754444R00052